STING

by STEVE GETT

Cherry Lane Books
P.O. BOX 430 ● PORT CHESTER, NY 10573

Cherry Lane Books, Port Chester, NY 10573
First printing
Printed in the United States of America

Editorial Direction by STEVE GETT
Art Direction and design by DAN RECCHIA
Front cover photograph by DANIEL QUATROCHI/RETNA
Production Coordination by FRANC GUERETTE

Library of Congress Cataloging in Publication Data

Gett, Steve, 1961–
   Sting.

   1. Sting (Musician)   2. Rock musicians—England—
Biography. I. Title.
ML419.S77C5 1985   784.5'4'00924 [B]   85-2612
ISBN 0-89524-281-8

Published by: Cherry Lane Books
            110 Midland Avenue
            Port Chester, NY 10573

PHOTO CREDITS:
All inside photos courtesy of Retna Ltd., except:
Kate Simon/Star File . . . . page 7
Bob Gruen/Star File . . . . page 33
Roger Johnson/Pix Int'l . . . . :. page 16

AN EVENING WITH STING

Dateline—February 25, 1985: As the midnight hour approached, the capacity crowd inside New York City's Ritz club was brimming with anticipation. Amidst a good deal of cheering, Sting walked onstage, clad in an oversized red jacket and baggy pants, with a Fender Telecaster hanging off his shoulder. Pausing momentarily to look out into the audience, he smiled and then eased his way into a mesmerizing solo rendition of *Roxanne*. Midway through the song, he was joined by saxophonist Branford Marsalis and two female back-up singers ... echoes of *Stop Making Sense?*

Upon completion of the opening number, the rest of Sting's band, which included bassist Darryl Jones and drummer Omar Hakim, emerged. The strong contingent of Police fans who were expecting to hear perhaps just one or two of the trio's tunes, were delighted when an uptempo version of *Shadows In The Rain* was unleashed.

After telling the crowd that he was "awfully nervous for some reason," Sting delivered another Police cut, *Driven To Tears*. He subsequently revealed that the rest of the set would include about five numbers that no one had ever heard before, the first of which was titled *Children's Crusade*—a song about "how the old abuse the young." Much to Sting's delight, the latter garnered extremely positive response from the crowd and was followed by *One World (Not Three)*.

The second "sneak preview" was a song about coalmining (possibly titled *Black Sea*) which heralded the introduction of a drum machine to the stage sound. Then, it was back to Police material: a funky version of *Bring On The Night* leading straight into *When The World Is Running Down, You Make The Best Of What's Still Around.*

Through his diligent selection of material, Sting had little difficulty in enticing the crowd to listen to his new compositions. A hush filled the venue as he explained that the next song was inspired by the Anne Rice novel *Interview With A Vampire.* He claimed that it was written under a full moon in the French Quarter of New Orleans and an acquaintance later reported that the title of the tune was *Moon Over Bourbon Street.*

After arming himself with "Brian"—his legendary stand-up bass—Sting declared that only a few people might know the next song, *I Burn For You.* However, judging by the enthusiastic audience response for the beautiful song, which was originally written back in 1976, Sting was forced to concede: "Well, obviously most of you *do* know it."

The final new number of the night was the uptempo *If You Love Somebody, Set Them Free,* after which came *Low Life*—"a very obscure old song." The main set finally came to a climax with the classic *Been Down So Long.*

Naturally, the crowd demanded an encore and Sting soon returned to play an unaccompanied version of *Message In A Bottle,* which provided him an excellent vehicle for his incredible vocal capabilities. Finally, the evening's entertainment was brought to a close with the old blues standard *Need Your Love So Bad.* As Sting left the stage, he was clearly well satisfied with his performance and said: "Thank you, thank you for coming. Bye-bye."

Sting spent the next two nights at the downtown Manhattan club, playing in front of sellout audiences, before leaving the Big Apple for Barbados, where he immediately started recording his debut solo album. The record is scheduled for a late spring release and is eagerly awaited by countless Sting devotees around the globe.

The author of this book will readily confess to being an ardent admirer of Sting's work. However, from the outset, it should be made quite clear that his aim was not to probe deeply into the entertainer's private life, but simply to document his history and attempt to supply fans with the most up-to-date analysis of his career.

There have been a number of rock biographies written about the Police, some good and some bad, but very few seem to have been presented with much care or thought. Sting himself was informed that this project was being undertaken and, although he was loathe to become directly involved, his personal photographer Daniel Quatrochi agreed to submit a number of candid pictures (including the spectacular cover shot), which had been approved by Sting. For this much, the author is extremely grateful. And, despite the fact that the research for the text basically revolved around gathering past interview material, one can only hope that Sting will acknowledge that the final product was written in good faith.

GROWING PAINS

Growing up in a working-class district of Northern England, Sting certainly never envisioned that one day he would be fronting a rock group that has sold in excess of 40 million albums; nor could he have forseen that he would end up appearing in a multi-million dollar movie like *Dune*. However, he always knew that he would go further than the mundane lifestyle of the environment in which he was raised.

Born on October 2, 1949 in Wallsend, Northumberland—a suburb of Newcastle—Gordon Matthew Sumner was the eldest of four children, with a brother, Philip, and sisters, Angela and Anita. The head of the household, Eric Sumner, forged a living as a milkman, while his wife was a hairdresser.

The Sumners lived on Gerald Street, near the river Tyne, and Sting has a stock story he seems to enjoy telling whenever he's asked about his childhood memories. When Bianca Jagger broached the subject, Sting told the former Rolling Stone wife: "I was brought up on a street of terraced houses and at the bottom of the street was a shipyard where they built tankers. And every year they built up this ship and at the end of the year it would vanish, it would go down into the river. Over the end of the street were these enormous great bows of a ship. I'll always remember that as being a primary image in my mind."

Like the giant vessels of the sea, young Gordon Sumner was destined to travel out into the great unknown. However, while a new ship would be launched from the docks of the Tyne every year, it would take time before the future Policeman embarked.

When he was six years old, Sting and his family moved to an apartment located above the dairy that his father ran on Station Road. It was also around this time that Sting began to take a keen interest in culture after reading a copy of Robert Louis Stevenson's classic novel *Treasure Island* during a visit to his grandmother, Agnes Sumner. She kept a healthy collection of books and magazines in her house, which Sting has since described as having "quite an intellectual atmosphere."

At the age of seven, Sting started making his first public appearances when he became an altar boy at St. Columba's Roman Catholic Church, for which he was required to learn the complete Latin service. Meanwhile, his natural feel for music was exhibited at home, where he would occasionally tickle the ivories of his mother's piano.

One of the major turning points in Sting's childhood came when he passed the "11-plus" examination, which enabled him to attend St. Cuthbert's grammar school. It should be mentioned that most youngsters from Sting's background received a basic government-funded education—going from a junior to a secondary modern school (the equivalent of the U.S. public school system). However, those who showed sufficient aptitude could be eligible for "direct grant" schools, which accepted both fee-paying students as well as a number of kids whose school fees were supported by funds from the local authorities. Sting fell into the latter category.

However, although he managed to get into the grammar school, life wasn't exactly a bed of roses for G. Sumner. For a start, he was so tall for his age (he claims that he was almost six-feet by the time he was nine) that the other pupils would call him "Lurch"—the name of the lanky butler in the Addams Family. Secondly, he was considered something of an outsider by the other local working-class kids who continued on the grim treadmill of the secondary modern school system.

By the time he was in his third year at St. Cuthbert's, Sting recalls that he had developed a strong rebellious streak. He has often talked about a master named Father Walsh, whose main role in life was to "strike the fear of God" into the pupils; mischievous lads would be on the receiving end of a few strokes of his cane. "It was most cruel, humiliating punishment ever," says Sting, who was caned for what he considered to be trivial things like arguing in class.

Discussing his school life with *Interview* magazine, he stated: "I think everyone who went to my school reacted to the reactionary regime that was down on us. In effect, I'm grateful for it because everybody became a little quirky, a little revolutionary; they wanted to fight against it. I'm not against it. I'm not against reactionary education, strict education."

During his grammar school days, Sting had begun to take a keen interest in the guitar, having acquired his first instrument from an uncle who had emigrated to Canada. He maintains that the Beatles were responsible for inspiring him to play and that they were his first major influence as both a songwriter and a musician.

Sting told writer John Duka that his musical drive came from himself and not from his parents. "They wanted me to wear a shirt and tie. But they weren't educated, so they had no knowledge that they could impart to me after the age of seven. I was hungry for it. I knew early on I could escape in music. They thought I was mad."

In past interviews, Sting has mentioned that his family life was fraught with tension

and that his parents often fought; it has been reported that Eric Sumner's marriage later ended in divorce. Sting once told a reporter that he had come from a family of losers and that he had rejected his family as something he didn't want to be like. However, on a subsequent encounter with the same journalist, he admitted that he had said a number of things that had hurt his family deeply. He reasoned that he had spoken out of arrogance and lack of thought.

Quite simply, one senses that breaking out of his background had been such a tough, bitter struggle that, once standing on the media soapbox, he had fallen prey to the press by airing his views so openly. One can sympathize with his dilemma. It almost seems as though, having made it to the top, Sting was determined to make it quite clear that he had achieved success under his own terms and on his own merit. He had discovered his own creative abilities and modes of expression by himself. Sure, there have been those who have inspired him en route, but essentially the fact that Sting had the desire to make something of his life came from his own inner self. Coming from a relatively "unexciting" background, with no one around to guide his future course, it is understandable that he should have gone through a phase of negativeness towards his background.

The very first live concert Sting attended was a Newcastle's Club A Go Go in 1965, where he witnessed the Graham Bond Organization, featuring legendary bassist Jack Bruce. The combination of seeing Bruce onstage, together with his self-confessed admiration for Paul McCartney, was probably the determining factor in Sting's decision to take up the bass. The following year, he was given his first four-string guitar by a friend named Pete Brigham.

Aside from the Beatles, Sting also became hooked on the black music that was emerging on the Motown and Stax labels. Eventually, he started listening to jazz records by the likes of Charlie Mingus and Thelonius Monk, as well as blues albums and even Bob Dylan's releases. However, he has since confessed that a lot of the music he got into was basically an effort to be "hip" and that he and his friends considered themselves to be somewhat elitist by their "avant-garde" musical tastes. During the mid-60's, Sting's literary horizons broadened as he discovered the beat novels of Jack Kerouac and such "nouveau" British poets as Ted Hughes and Philip Larkin.

In the summer of 1969, Sting finally left school with the intention of going on to university if his grades were good enough. He took a part-time job working as a bus conductor in Newcastle, before finding out that he had scored A-level certificates in economics, geography and English. His grades were no more than average, but they were enough for him to gain acceptance at Warwick University, which is located in the British midlands, near Coventry.

University didn't work out for Sting though, and consequently he soon found himself traveling back north to live with his parents. It was an unsettling period and he ended up spending the next six months working on a building site. He then secured a civil service job with the Inland Revenue. He hated working there and, unable to conform to the system, he quit after continually being threatened with the sack.

Finally, Sting decided to apply for a position at the Northern Counties Teacher Training College, just outside Newcastle. He was accepted and started his course in the fall of 1971, studying for a teachers' certificate in English and music.

Music still held a strong place in Sting's heart and he often found himself frequenting the Newcastle pub scene, where a lot of jazz bands would play. At the teacher training college, he met a keyboard player named Gerry Richardson. A friend of Gerry's had apparently seen Sting playing James Taylor songs at a folk club; it wasn't long before Sting and Richardson had joined forces with a drummer and a horn section to form the band Earthrise. Although their group was never destined to set the world on fire, the two would-be-teachers became close friends. Gerry occasionally gigged with the Phoenix trad jazz band and subsequently Sting played with them. According to numerous sources, it was the trombone player who was responsible for giving Gordon Sumner the name Sting, when the young bassist had worn a yellow and black soccer shirt. One version of the story claims that the nickname was originally "Stinger" but that it was eventually shortened to just plain "Sting."

Sting soon garnered a strong reputation for his playing and, during the early 70's, he worked in a variety of outfits, including the River City Jazzmen and the Newcastle Big Band. In order to play with the latter group, Sting had to learn to read music. Within six weeks he had taught himself and claims that he found music easy to learn because "it's quite a logical mathematical process."

It was during his stint with the Newcastle Big Band that Sting made his first record. Titled simply THE NEWCASTLE BIG BAND, one side was cut at the University Theatre—the group's main local gigspot—while the other was recorded at the Pau jazz festival in the south of France. Two thousand copies were pressed, which were sold at concerts.

Reflecting on his early days as a gigging

musician, Sting has said that he played a variety of styles: Dixieland, mainstream, be-bop, free-form and in a big band. However, despite the fact that bands like Deep Purple and Led Zeppelin had become increasingly popular, heavy rock held absolutely no in-terest for Sting. He has since referred to it as "turgid, pompous and arrogant."

Far more appealing to Sting were jazz-rock fusion outfits like Return To Forever and Weather Report, whose lineups boasted the incredible bass talents of Stanley Clarke and Jaco Pastorius, respectively. Sting once described Pastorius as "probably the greatest bass player alive; he makes me want to give up!"

Sting was completely converted to the Pastorius/Clarke style when he played a gig with the Big Band at Newcastle Polytechnic opening for Return To Forever. He claims that seeing Stanley Clarke in action totally altered his musical way of thinking.

Gerry Richardson was equally im-pressed. Consequently, he and Sting decided to put their own jazz group together, which they called Last Exit—a name reportedly inspired by Hubert Selby Jr.'s novel *Last Exit to Brooklyn*. Playing a mixture of Chick Corea songs, soul covers and Gerry/Sting compo-sitions, the band initially started off doing small gigs, but it wasn't long before they had amassed a sizeable following on the New-castle scene.

Although it might seem that Sting was wholeheartedly dedicating himself to music, he was still going through his three-year teacher training course. After graduating in the summer of 1974, he took a job at a primary school in Cramlington, a small min-ing village about 10 miles north of Newcastle. During his training course, he had taught teenagers at secondary schools, but at Cram-lington he found himself guiding five-to 10-year-olds. He has confided that he liked the kids but isn't too sure that he actually accomplished much as a teacher since his main aim was for them to enjoy themselves.

When British music critic Paul Morley asked Sting if he felt that teaching served as a good apprenticeship for going out onstage with a rock group, he replied: "Yeah, learning to stand up in front of people and not being an arsehole, although I might seem to be one. Self-confidence in front of people. En-tertaining, I suppose. I think the phenomenon in the classroom isn't teaching, it's learning. I think what you have to do is create an atmosphere where people can feel happy and want to learn things, and I think the rock'n'roll thing is similar. You create an atmosphere where people can let themselves go, get worked up if you like. It's a sort of ritualized release. We get back to the placebo thing: wouldn't they be better off on the streets, being down on the government, killing off old ladies? I don't know. Music made me give up teaching."

Aside from graduating in 1974, Sting

finally left home and moved into an apartment with a friend, actor Newton Willis, in the east Newcastle borough of Jesmond.

In December 1974, Last Exit got a gig at the University Theatre for a Christmas show, written by British pop veteran Tony Hatch, called *Rock Nativity*. Playing the role of the Virgin Mary was an Irish lass named Frances Tomelty, the daughter of actor Jo-seph Tomelty. Suffice to say, Sting and Frances hit it off immediately. When the show's run ended, she went back to London and sub-sequently worked in various provincial thea-ters, as well as starring in a children's TV show called *No Place To Hide*. However, despite the fact that they were both busy, Sting and Frances saw each other whenever they could.

Last Exit continued to gig and, aside from appearing at a Spanish jazz festival in San Sebastian, they also performed on a

---

---

cruise. Throughout 1975, the group spent a good deal of time recording demos at Impulse Studios in Wallsend. These sessions resulted in the release of a single *Whispering Voices,* which was written by Gerry Richardson and sung by Sting. Several hundred copies of a nine-track cassette Lp were later issued under the title FIRST FROM LAST EXIT. The featured material included a number of Sting compositions: *We Got Something, Carrion Prince, On This Train, Oh My God, Truth Kills* and *Savage Beast.*

Although Last Exit had initially begun life as a jazz group, Sting had eventually started writing songs and singing them. "The fact that I can sing is an accident of genetics," he once proclaimed. However, he maintains that he had a naturally high voice and that he listened to female singers like Cleo Laine and Flora Purim, although he never tried to model himself on them.

Sting's relationship with Frances To-

melty had continued to grow and finally, on May 1, 1976, the couple tied the knot at St. Oswins Roman Catholic Church in Tyne-mouth. Frances soon began to take a keener interest in Sting's musical career and she shopped some of their demo tapes around London. As he continued to come up with new songs, Sting took over control of the group; the jazz fusion roots had made way for a more straightforward pop approach. Be that as it may, none of the record companies was interested in signing Last Exit.

Although Sting had written a tune called *Don't Give Up Your Daytime Job,* he quit his teaching job in the summer of '76, despite the fact that Frances was pregnant and was due to give birth in November. By now, he was determined to forge a full-time career in music.

Last Exit were finding it tough to get a break, though, since a recording contract continued to elude them. However they did manage to secure a publishing deal. Carol Wilson of Virgin Music had persuaded the company's boss, Richard Branson, and a number of others to go and see the band in Newcastle. Although the label wasn't pre-pared to take on the group as a recording act, Ms. Wilson recognized Sting's writing potential and snapped up the publishing rights to his material. It wasn't exactly a great deal and in fact Sting would later regret signing with Virgin.

Carol Wilson subsequently organized a showcase gig for Last Exit at London's Ding-walls club. Only a handful of people showed up, but it sparked off some media interest from the British music weekly *Sounds.* On their way back to Newcastle, the group stopped off at London's Pathway studios to record some more demos and it was at this juncture that they decided that they would have to move down to the capital if they were to make any headway.

On November 23, 1976, Frances Tomelty gave birth to a son, Joseph. However, both parents had agreed that they still wanted to continue with their individual careers. Sting has said that he never wanted to have to tell his son, "I gave up the best years of my life for you." Even though he now had a wife *and* son to support, nothing was going to stop him from attempting to make it.

By mid-December, Last Exit were only committed to a couple of local gigs, which included a Christmas concert at St. Mary's Teacher Training College. That same night, a moderately unsuccessful British band called Curved Air, featuring American drummer Stewart Copeland, happened to be in New-castle. After their show, Copeland was per-suaded to go and check out Last Exit. Al-though he wasn't particularly impressed by the band, he was knocked out by Sting's outstanding stage presence.

That chance sighting was to eventually lead to the start of something big—the for-mation of the Police.

WALKING THE BEAT

Since this book is primarily concerned with Sting, it seems rather unnecessary to devote too much attention to Stewart Copeland's background. The third son of Miles Copeland II—a one-time jazz trumpeter, former army intelligence officer and ex-CIA agent—Stewart became hooked on music from an early age. After his brothers, Ian and Miles, both became involved in the business, it was only a matter of time before young Stewart followed in their footsteps. Although he showed a marked flair for the drums as a youngster, he actually worked as a roadie, manager and tour manager, before he became a member of the group Curved Air.

When Stewart saw Sting playing with Last Exit in Newcastle, Curved Air were very much on their last legs. By the end of 1976, Stewart had quit the band.

However, far from being a somewhat disillusioned "ex-member of a band," Stewart found himself eager to start afresh, having been inspired by the punk uprising, which was spearheaded by groups like the Sex Pistols and the Damned. The American drummer was excited by their raw energy and "let's-break-the-rules" attitudes towards music. He came up with a name for his own punk band—the Police—and immediately started looking for accompanying musicians.

Meanwhile, at the beginning of 1977, Sting had decided to follow his gut feeling and make the permanent move to London. Arriving in the capital with nowhere to live, Sting and his family temporarily took up residence with one of Frances' friends, an agent named Pippa Markham. Times were hard and they were forced to sleep on the floor. Still, it was a base.

Although Gerry Richardson had also traveled down to London, the other members of Last Exit were uncertain about making such a dramatic move. Eventually, they plucked up enough courage to hit the big city and the group got together for a series of London pub gigs. However, in a matter of weeks, the band split up, with all of the members, except Sting and Gerry, returning to Newcastle.

Sting had been prepared to give Last Exit a last shot, but in the meantime he had also started rehearsing with Stewart Copeland. When the drummer had initially con-

"My real name IS Sting. The name I was given when I was born was Gordon Matthew Sumner, but I had no choice in that matter. I did have a choice in Sting, therefore, I think my real name is Sting."
—Interview, 1982

sidered approaching Sting to join his band, he wasn't aware that the former school-teacher was already on his way down to London. As soon as he arrived, the two musicians had started rehearsing together at Copeland's apartment.

Despite the fact that he had managed to recruit Sting's services, Stewart faced a tough task in getting a suitable guitarist for the group. While most of the punks had an enthusiastic attitude, they tended to lack ability as far as their instruments were concerned; at the same time, serious-minded musicians weren't prepared to compromise their style by playing what they deemed to be a crude, basic form of music.

Enter 24-year-old, Corsican born strummer, Henri Padovani, with whom Stewart had become acquainted during Curved Air's last days. Padovani went up to the band's final gig at St. Albans in December '76 and subsequently Stewart took him to see the Damned at London's infamous punk club, the

Roxy. Before long, the guitarist had cut his hair, shaved off his beard and taken on a new wave image. His musical talents may have been limited, but as far as Stewart was concerned, at least he had a band.

By the second week of February—before they had even played a gig—the Police were at Pathway Studios, recording two songs, which were to be released as an independent single. The A-side was a Stewart composition entitled *Fall Out,* while the flipside, *Nothing Achieving,* was written by the drummer and his brother Ian. Henri Padovani's guitar playing was apparently so poor that Stewart ended up handling the lead work.

A month later, the Police embarked on their first set of live dates, hooking up with American "punk" starlet—and David Bowie's former publicist—Cherry Vanilla. An agreement was set up that the Police would be the opening act and, since Ms. Vanilla was only able to bring her guitarist over from the States, Stewart and Sting would also accom-

pany her on stage.

Towards the end of March, the Police traveled to Holland as an opening act for Wayne County and the Electric Chairs. They also played a gig with Billy Idol's Generation X and the Jam, before returning to England for another stint with Cherry Vanilla at the beginning of April.

May saw the release of *Fall Out* on Stewart Copeland's own Illegal Records label. Subsequently, the Police played their first headline show at a pub called the Railway Hotel in Putney, south London. There were other occasional dates at clubs like the Hope and Anchor, but the group failed to generate any significant kind of interest.

During their early gigging days, most of the Police's live set comprised Stewart Copeland material. Sting managed to sneak in a few of his tunes, including *Don't Give Up Your Daytime Job.* As he recalled to rock scribe Jon Pidgeon: "It was largely Stewart's material in the beginning, but as time went on I found that I wanted to say more. I wanted to use my voice better, so I started writing material in that mold, but one problem I kept coming up against all the time in my writing was the limitations of our guitarist.''

Sting has openly admitted that he didn't think much of Stewart Copeland's songs when he joined the group and that it was the drummer's energy that impressed him. However, from the outset, one thing he had never been able to come to terms with was Henri Padovani's guitar playing.

He was also uncomfortable with the band's association with the punk movement and felt that they had little in common with the spikey-topped rebels. At one early Police gig, Sting came up with his now infamous comment, "Alright—we're going to play some punk now, which means that the lyrics are banal and the music's terrible . . ." The Police were not "punk" and according to Sting: "Our involvement was really a flag of convenience. The only thing we shared with those people was a felling of energy and wanting to overturn things.''

Despite the emergence of *Fall Out,* the Police had begun to find themselves in a rut and Stewart Copeland knew that he would have to be very careful not to let Sting drift away. Gerry Richardson had become the musical director for Billy Ocean (who recently topped the charts with *Carribbean Queen*) and, knowing that Sting wasn't totally satisfied with the Police, he offered him a gig in the soul singer's band. Although it would have provided him with a steady wage, Sting decided to continue working with Stewart.

One thing was very clear though: Henri Padovani had to be given his marching orders if the Police were to make progress.

However, before Padovani was given the proverbial boot, Sting was contacted by former Gong bassist Mike Howlett, who asked him to play in a band called Strontium 90 for a one-off Gong reunion in Paris. Howlett agreed to take Stewart along as his drummer, but he wasn't interested in Padovani, since he had already armed himself with a guitarist named Andy Summers.

Andy Summers had actually been working professionally for over a decade; after making his first appearance on a record with Zoot Money in 1964, he had gone on to enjoy stints with a variety of acts, including Soft Machine, Kevin Ayers, the Animals and Kevin Coyne. His first confrontation with Sting and Stewart took place in May '77 at a London rehearsal studio, where they prepared a live set with Mike Howlett for the Strontium 90 gig. The Gong reunion took place at the end of the month and was held in a huge circus tent.

Strontium 90 later played a date at London's Nashville Rooms, where they were billed as the Elevators. However, that was to be their last live performance. The group's only legacy was a single, titled *Nuclear Waste*, which featured Sting on lead vocals.

Upon their return to Britain, the Police had started gigging again. Andy Summers popped down to see them at the Marquee Club one night and got onstage for a jam during the encore. Andy was swift to recognize the band's potential beyond the limitations of punk and a few days later he telephoned Sting, suggesting that he should become part of the Police force. Sting had enjoyed playing with a "proper" guitarist and, in view of his feelings towards Henri Padovani, was open to the idea. It wasn't long before Andy had convinced Stewart that he was the right man for the job. However, he agreed to join on one condition: the Police continue to function as a trio.

The process of eliminating Henri Padovani was delayed, owing to the fact that the Police were already committed to a couple

"(The Police) is not an easy relationship by any means. We're three highly autonomous individuals, and a band is an artificial alliance most of the time. There are obviously tensions, but I think there's a great love between us and a genuine respect. I can't think of two musicians I'd rather play with. But none of us is easy to work with. It's not all buddy-buddy, and never was."
—*Rolling Stone, 1983*

of projects. Aside from an upcoming appearance at a French punk rock festival, a recording session had also been scheduled. Consequently, it was decided that Padovani would be kicked out as soon as they had finished working in the studio.

During the interim period, the Police carried on working as a four-piece. On August 6, 1977, they played their final gig with Padovani at the Mont de Marson punk festival in the south of France. The subsequent recording session turned out to be something of a nightmare. The band had enlisted former Velvet Underground member John Cale as a producer, but it soon became clear that they had made a mistake. Cale was intrigued by the punk scene and he actually favored Henri Padovani's guitar work over Andy Summers' playing. The straw that broke the camel's back came when the producer reportedly argued vehemently with Sting over the vocals for a song called *Visions In The Night*. It was only a matter of days before Padovani had left the group and returned to his native Corsica. Ironically enough, he ended up joining Wayne County's Electric Chairs, whom the Police had supported on their inaugural European dates.

With Padovani out of the way, Andy Summers was in a far better position to make his presence felt. Furthermore, Sting's

enthusiasm was instantly rekindled. Stewart told one British writer: "One by one, Sting's songs had started coming in and, because he's a good writer and they're really good stuff, you can't just turn them down. When Andy joined the group, it opened up new numbers of Sting's we could do now, so the material started to get a lot more interesting and Sting started to take a lot more interest in the group."

After a few rehearsals, the Police made their debut as a trio on August 18, 1977 at Rebecca's Club in Birmingham. However, due to their association with the punk movement (which had died down considerably) they found it hard to get other live work. In October, the band traveled to Europe for a series of opening dates with the Damned. They also managed to secure the support slot with Wayne County in Paris and it was reportedly during their stay in the French capital that Sting came up with the song *Roxanne*.

The inspiration allegedly came from a late-night wander through the city's red light district, where Sting witnessed prostitution on the streets for the first time. He claims that he thought some of the girls were beautiful and that he began to wonder what it would be like to be in love with a hooker. When asked how he came up with the title

Roxanne, he told one reporter that he considered it a beautiful name; that there was such a rich mythology behind it and that it had been the name of Alexander the Great's wife and Cyrano de Bergerac's girlfriend.

The Paris gig was actually the final date on the band's brief European trip. Sting immediately returned to England, while Stewart and Andy went off to Munich to work with German artist Ebehard Schoener. Prior to joining the Police, the guitarist had agreed to record an Lp with Schoener and he managed to get Stewart involved in the project. Shortly after the two musicians arrived in Munich, Sting received a phone call asking him to come over and join them.

The trio spent three weeks working in Germany before they flew back to London. Despite their lack of gigging on the home front, the *Fall Out* single had notched up impressive sales—10,000 copies had been sold—and so the band decided to record an album. According to Stewart, they would only have to sell 5,000 copies in order to cover their costs, which seemed a "realistic target."

Yet, although the group had earned money from working with Ebehard Schoener, times were still hard. During these early days, the members were often forced to turn to their wives or girlfriends for support. Sting was fortunate that Frances continued to secure acting parts. Indeed, one of her jobs— a role in the television series *The Survivors*— had called for the on-camera presence of a baby; Frances had been swift to offer the services of Sting's son Joseph.

Sting himself managed to get modeling work through Pippa Markham, the friend who had provided his family with sleeping quarters when he first came down to London. As a result, he appeared in advertisements for men's necklaces, denim jeans and brassieres. He also auditioned for the role of a "punk" in a Wrigley's chewing gum commercial. After landing the part, he discovered that the director actually wanted to employ a band and so he managed to get Stewart and Andy involved. The one stipulation was that the whole group had to have blond hair. No objections were raised, and that's how the Police stumbled on their trademark blond image.

But acting in TV commercials wasn't going to cover the cost of recording an Lp, so towards the end of 1977 Stewart approached his brother Miles to see if he would be prepared to provide the necessary financial backing. Although Miles hadn't exactly been impressed by the group's track record to date, he agreed to help out. Studio time was booked to commence early in the new year.

IS THERE
LIFE
AFTER A LAWSCHOOL
MORE CHOWDER BOYS
SMAGMA

RED LIGHT SUCCESS

At the beginning of January, 1978, Sting journeyed back to Newcastle for a hometown reunion with his old band Last Exit. It was the first live performance in over two months and, although he enjoyed getting up onstage again, he had more important matters on his mind. The Police had arranged to start recording their debut Lp on January 13 at Surrey Sound Studios in Leatherhead, England.

The 16-track studio was run by Nigel Gray, a former doctor who had give up his practice to pursue a musical career, with the cooperation of his brother Chris. The band had chosen the place because the rooms had a strong natural sound and also because the rates were particularly reasonable. Miles Copeland had negotiated a deal whereby he would either pay Nigel Gray, who was also responsible for the production, a set fee when the album was finished or a percentage if he was prepared to wait. Since the Grays had injected a good deal of money into the studio, having converted it from an old theater, Nigel opted to take the cash. However, he later claimed that Miles kept him waiting for his check and that he might just as well have taken the percentage point.

Miles made sporadic trips to Surrey Sound during the recording sessions. Word has it that he wasn't particularly impressed by the band's progress until he popped down in mid-March and heard *Roxanne* for the first time. Totally knocked out by the song, he took a tape to A&M Records the following day and persuaded them to release it as a single. Miles was on extremely good terms with the label since he also managed Squeeze, who had already enjoyed a couple of hits. However, rather than accept any money for *Roxanne*, he secured a higher royalty rate for the group, which meant that they stood to make more cash if the record was a hit and were also under no obligation to pay back any advances. Miles also committed A&M to release *Roxanne* in America.

With these feats accomplished, it was only a matter of time before Miles Copeland became the band's official manager. *Roxanne* hit British record stores in early April and, although it garnered favorable press reviews, it received very little radio airplay. Much to

Sting's annoyance, the DJ's and program directors at the BBC (the top U.K. radio network) considered that a love song directed towards a prostitute was unsuitable for their listening audience.

Due to the lack of radio exposure, the Police found it tougher than ever to get live bookings. They played one gig with Steel Pulse at London's Roundhouse at the end of April, but then returned to Germany to spend three weeks working with Eberhard Schoener's Laser Theater.

When the Police returned to England in June, they discovered that *Roxanne* had failed to register any significant chart impact and

had "died." However, the record hadn't gone completely unnoticed and a number of music industry people (including Mick Jagger) had picked up on it.

A&M issued a second single, *Can't Stand Losing You,* on August 14, but once again the Police ran into problems with the BBC, who objected to the suicide angle of the lyrics—not to mention the photograph on the picture sleeve, which depicted Sting hanging from a noose, his feet supported by a block of ice, which was slowly being melted by an electric fire. Sting claimed that the BBC had vetoed the song because the lyrics contained the word 'kill,' which he found most aggravating since there had been a number of hit songs written about suicide in the history of pop music. He maintained that he had used the angle in a tongue-in-cheek sense.

Despite the controversy that had surrounded the singles, A&M decided to go ahead and pick up their option to release the first Police album, which was finally completed in August and had been titled OUTLANDOS D'AMOUR. Since the record had been self-financed, the trio received a healthy check from the label when they handed over the master tapes.

Meanwhile, in September, Sting started working on his first movie, *Quadrophenia,* based on the Who's double Lp about the violent mods-and-rockers confrontations that had occurred in Britain during the mid-60's. Sting's wife Frances had told him that casting sessions were being held, but he was initially wary about auditioning. However, he eventually got together with director Franc Roddam and made a sufficiently good impression to land the part of Ace Face—the "Brighton wide-boy with the best mohair suit, full-length leather coat, and smartest Vespa scooter." During the rehearsals, Sting learned to ride a scooter, as well as the steps to several popular 60's dances.

Activity on the Police front may have been limited for a couple of months, but Sting was still totally committed to the band. Upon his return from the film world, he found himself preparing to embark on a series of U.S. concerts, which Miles Copeland had arranged. A&M Records thought that it would be crazy for the Police to play American dates at this juncture and weren't prepared to provide any financial backing. That didn't

"I just wanted to see what it was like to stop eating meat, so I stopped about six weeks ago and now the thought of eating a steak or a hamburger revolts me. It's very strange. I never had that feeling before. But I feel healthy enough."

—TV interview on the set of *The Bride*, 1984

bother Miles though and his only request was that *Roxanne* be made available in record stores and distributed to radio stations throughout the country.

A low-budget itinerary was set up and, on October 20, the band flew to New York on Freddie Laker's Skytrain. The flight didn't arrive at JFK airport until 11 p.m., but an hour later the Police were onstage at CBGB's playing the first of two shows at the legendary downtown Manhattan club. Accompanied by Kim Turner, whose work covered everything from tour management to sound engineering, the group toured on the East Coast, playing 23 shows in less than a month.

Miles Copeland had a strategy that the trio would always headline in the States— even if it meant playing to just a handful of people in a club. Sting has vivid recollections of one such gig in Poughkeepsie, which coincided with Monday night football. The audience comprised three people: the bartender and two others! Although it was a trifle embarrassing, the group played the show with an attitude of "no matter how many people are out there—let's give it all we've got." One member of the Poughkeepsie gathering happened to be a DJ, who immediately started spinning *Roxanne* on his turntable.

The American dates ended with another two-night stand at CBGB's, by which time *Roxanne* was beginning to make headway on the U.S. charts. Shortly after the group returned to Britain, OUTLANDOS D'AMOUR hit the streets.

<table>
<tr><td>

OUTLANDOS D'AMOUR
Side One:
Next To You
So Lonely
Roxanne
Hole In My Life
Peanuts
Side Two:
Can't Stand Losing You
Truth Hits Everybody
Born In The 50's
Be My Girl—Sally
Masoko Tanga

</td></tr>
</table>

Of the 10 tracks on the Lp, eight were penned by Sting; he collaborated with Andy on *Be My Girl* and with Stewart on *Peanuts*. In a 1981 British radio interview, Sting was asked about the distinction between his old group Last Exit and the Police and he assessed: "The jump was bridged by records like *Fall Out* and being a pseudo punk group which we weren't. The difference between *Roxanne* and Last Exit wasn't that big. The difference between *Fall Out* and Last Exit was enormous. I went back to being melodic and owning up that I wasn't punk. I was an ex-schoolteacher. *Roxanne* was one my favorites."

Towards the end of November, 1978, the Police performed at London's Electric Ballroom. A few weeks later, they embarked on a series of U.K. gigs, opening for the satirical rock group Alberto Y Lost Trios Paranoias. More often than not, they reportedly blew the headlining act offstage, with a lot of fans turning up to see them on the strength of their two A&M singles. Finally, the Police were starting to gain momentum.

At the beginning of 1979, the trio returned to Germany for another set of concerts with Ebehard Schoener. Some of their work with Schoener emerged on two German albums; an Lp, titled VIDEO FLASHBACK, was also released in the U.K.

By late January, Sting, Stewart and Andy were back at Surrey Sound Studios

working on their second album. The facilities had been upgraded to accomodate 24-track recording, but the band still managed to keep their costs to a minimum. With the profits from OUTLANDOS, they were able to pay their own way and thus avoided coming under the control of the record company. Once again, they would also stand to make more money by delivering finished product to the label.

February saw the Police setting off on their second visit to America, where they promoted OUTLANDOS, which was released in the U.S. at the end of the month. A special police badge-shaped picture disc of *Roxanne* was also issued. The band traveled from coast-to-coast during the 30-date tour, which came to a close in early April with a free concert in Philadelphia. Playing live shows in America helped to push both *Roxanne* and OUTLANDOS up the charts.

Interest in the band had continued to mount back home in Britain, where *Roxanne* was reissued in the second week of April. Following an appearance on the weekly TV music show *Top Of The Pops,* the single reached number 12. Sting told one reporter that he knew that the Police had "arrived" when he was lying in a hotel bed and a window washer started whistling *Roxanne.* OUTLANDOS D'AMOUR also appeared on the U.K. charts—six months after its initial release!

Eager to capitalize on their American success, the Police flew off for a third U.S. tour at the end of April. Upon their return to Britain, the trio's hectic pace continued with U.K. headlining dates in June. They had escalated from playing small clubs to performing at the country's larger venues and most of the shows were sold out. The live set was basically centered around the debut Lp, with *Message In A Bottle* thrown in as a sneak preview.

Although the sessions for the second album were completed by the beginning of August, A&M had decided to re-release *Can't Stand Losing You* in Britain. The band may have felt that it was a case of "1978 revisited" but the idea paid off when the song rocketed to the number two position.

After a series of European headlining shows, the Police came back to Britain, where they topped the Friday night bill at the Reading Festival—an annual three-day event on the U.K. music calendar—on August 24. Before they went onstage, they were presented with various album and singles awards in the A&M Records' hospitality tent.

Police mania had begun to sweep through Britain and, naturally, Sting was the focus for a good deal of media attention. *Quadrophenia* opened in movie theaters and it turned out that Sting's role as Ace Face was actually

a silent part. However, he still earned favorable reviews for his performance. He maintains that he was on the screen "enough to make an impression and short enough not to blow it."

1979 also witnessed Sting's cameo appearance in the film *Radio On.* He played the part of a garage mechanic who idolizes Eddie Cochran and, during his three-minutes in front of the camera, spends most of his time sitting in a caravan doorway strumming an acoustic rendition of Cochran's *Three Steps To Heaven.* Other roles were offered and Sting is believed to have declined invitations to star in a Francis Ford Coppola production and to play a villain in the James Bond film *For Your Eyes Only.* He did, however, allow himself to get roped into the Sex Pistols' *Great Rock'n'Roll Swindle* flick, but fortunately his scenes were edited out before the (so-called) film was released.

At this stage, Sting's involvement with the movie world was minor and his main concern was the success of the Police. Shortly after their triumphant performance at the Reading Festival, *Message In A Bottle* emerged. It was soon followed by the eagerly anticipated second Lp, REGGATTA DE BLANC.

REGGATTA DE BLANC
Side One:
Message In A Bottle
Reggatta de Blanc
It's Alright For You
Bring On The Night
Deathwish
Side Two:
Walking On The Moon
On Any Other Day
The Bed's Too Big Without You
Contact
Does Everybody Stare
No Time This Time

The Lp immediately raced to the top of the British charts and the Police were lauded for their style, which was loosely described as "an excellent blend of rock and reggae." Sting has often said that he was never a particularly ardent reggae supporter, claim-ing that he had simply been an admirer of black artists in general—everyone from James Brown to Bob Marley. He has denied being any kind of "rasta-maniac" but, of Marley, he once confided: "I'm not a fan by any means of anybody's. But the sense of loss I experienced when the man died was indescribable. I really felt we'd lost somebody great because he was such a width of talent. He could write political songs, love songs, silly pop songs . . ."

Coinciding with the release of REGGATTA DE BLANC, the Police kicked off another British headlining tour, which included two shows at London's Hammersmith Odeon at the end of September. Immediately afterwards, the band set off on their fourth North American tour. Despite the fact that the first wave of the Police's success had started in the U.S., the initial interest had subsided. Both *Message In A Bottle* and REGGATTA DE BLANC had received fairly lukewarm response. Nevertheless, the group spent the entire months of October and November on the road trying to stir things up. Midway through the tour, they were informed that *Walking On The Moon* had topped the British singles charts. Sting had apparently come up with the song in a Munich hotel when he was a little worse the wear for alcohol. He originally started humming the tune with the words "walking round the room"—after sobering up, he put the song together properly and titled it *Walking On The Moon*.

The U.S. trek finally ground to a halt on December 1. The following day, the trio jetted off to Paris for the start of a brief European jaunt. On December 10, a series of British gigs commenced, all of which attracted capacity crowds. The band actually performed two London concerts—at the Hammersmith Odeon and the Hammersmith Palais—in one night, with an armoured vehicle transporting them between the two venues. The pre-Christmas dates finally climaxed in Lewisham with a charity benefit in aid of the Dr. Barnados children's homes, where the cost of a ticket was a toy.

Over the past three years, Sting had been transformed from a frustrated jazz musician to leading one of Britain's top rock acts. By the end of 1979, the Police had reportedly sold five million singles and two million albums around the world. And this was only the beginning . . .

WORLD DOMINATION

Although the Police had already spent four months on the road promoting REGGATTA DE BLANC, Miles Copeland wasn't prepared to allow the group's pace to slacken. In January, 1980, there was another U.S. tour, which took the band through the Midwest and along the Northwest coast, and

> *"What comes out that surprises me is that people see me as arrogant. To a certain extent, I am, but any artist worth his salt has arrogance. It's a prerequisite of being stageworthy. You have to have a certain air of 'watch me, because I'm really good.' But I'm quite humble in many ways (laughing)— sclf-cffacing and modest."*
> **—Rolling Stone, 1983**

ended at the beginning of February with a date at the University of Hawaii in Honolulu. Subsequently, they embarked on a global onslaught that included concerts in a wide variety of interesting and exotic places.

Kicking off with seven Japanese dates, the trio then flew south for two shows at Today's World Disco in Hong Kong. The latter venue only held 400 people and both gigs drcw capacity crowds. Unfortunately, Sting contracted a throat infection during the band's stay in Hong Kong and by the time they arrived in New Zealand, he was barely able to sing. He managed to get through the first date in Christchurch, but the rest of the New Zealand dates had to be cancelled.

When the Police reached Australia in early March, Sting's health had improved and they were able to continue with their itinerary. While they were "down under" the group recorded a new song called *Driven To Tears* at a studio in Melbourne. Immediately

after the final Aussie date in Perth, the Police set off to India, where they became the first ever rock group to perform in Bombay, with two shows on March 25 and 26.

The Indian concerts were organized by the Time and Talents Club of Bombay—basically a group of old ladies, whose usual function was running more low-key events such as jumble sales. The band played at a 5,000 seat open-air arena in the center of the city and raised over $10,000 for sick children. Most of the tickets were bought by the upper-class citizens of Bombay but, after a series of mini-riots, the lower-class element came charging in. Sting told the people that the Police played "dance music" and soon had them enthusiastically jumping up and down. He later confessed that Bombay was the most rewarding gig of his career and claimed: "I'll never do a better one—that confirmed my belief in music as a universal phenomenon that can work anywhere."

A few days later, the Police arrived in Cairo, Egypt, for a show at the American University, which Sting is unlikely ever to forget. During the set, he became increasingly peeved at one fellow who was throwing the fans back in their seats in an extremely rough manner. Sting hurled a few insults at the man, who turned out to be the head of the Cairo police force.

After the show, Miles Copeland came backstage saying that the official was demanding an apology. Sting refused to comply with his manager's pleas and when the man entered the dressing room, he grabbed his bag and started to walk out. The police chief immediately followed him. Sting soon realized that if he didn't say anything, he would probably wind up in prison. He tried to say sorry, but couldn't bring himself to get the words out. Miles Copeland instantly intervened and convinced the man that Sting was attempting to apologize. The official was content and walked away declaring that the singer was a "man of honor."

The moral of that little story, according to Sting, is that he finds it impossible to accept someone else's "ascendancy and power."

At the end of March, the Police played two concerts in Athens, Greece, and became the first western rock band to perform in the country since the Rolling Stones during the late 60's. Over the next few weeks their globetrotting stint continued through Europe with dates in Italy, France, Spain, Belgium, Holland and West Germany.

The Police's 1980 world tour finally ended in May with two charity concerts in Newcastle, with all of the proceeds given to the Northumberland Association of Boys' Clubs. Although he was happy to raise the money, Sting wasn't altogether satisfied with the gigs in his old hometown. He felt that because the tickets had only been available by postal application, only the most "efficient" people had got them and consequently the crowd response was somewhat laid-back.

Sting's next public performance was at London's Notre Dame Hall, where he jammed with the band Chelsea during the songs *Right To Work, Trouble Is The Day* and *Urban Kids.*

In June, he was forced to take up residence in Eire in order to avoid paying excessive taxes to the British government if he continued to live in the U.K. Sting wasn't adverse to the move, owing to the fact that he needed some peace and quiet to write songs for the next Police album.

A&M Records had been hoping to release the band's third Lp in the summer of 1980. When the label's U.K. division realized that this wouldn't be possible, they decided to repackage all of the trio's past singles, together with a new version of *The Bed's Too Big Without You* (b/w a live version of *Truth Hits Everybody*), and put them out in blue vinyl. The set of seven-inch records, which came in a plastic folder, was limited to a pressing of 58,000 copies. The retail price was almost six pounds and the British press expressed concern that die-hard Police fans were being exploited by having to fork out for recordings that they already owned. The band members weren't exactly happy and one could hardly blame them for the problem, since the release was beyond their control.

Meanwhile, Sting was facing the tough task of coming up with a brand new set of songs. On both OUTLANDOS D'AMOUR and REGGATTA DE BLANC, he had been able to rely on tunes that he had written before he joined the band. A lot of his early Police songs were rooted in Last Exit compositions. *So Lonely* stemmed from a tune called *Fool In Love; Bring On The Night* was originally called *Carrion Prince,* the title of which had been taken from a Ted Hughes poem called *King of Carrion.* The subject matter of *Carrion Prince* concerned itself with Pontius Pilate. However, after Sting acquainted himself with Gary Gilmore's story in Norman Mailer's book *The Executioner's Song,* the number took on a new perspective. Indeed, Sting has revealed that he sang *Bring On The Night* with Gary Gilmore in mind.

During the Police's 1979–80 REGGATTA DE BLANC tour, the only new song injected into the set had been *Driven To Tears.* One could be excused for assuming that Sting was inspired to write the tune after he'd visited places like Bombay, but he maintains he was actually influenced by seeing television and newspaper coverage of death in the Third World.

Since the Police were unable to record

in Britain for tax reasons, they traveled to Wisseloord Studio in Hilversum, Holland at the beginning of July. The sessions, which were once again produced by Nigel Gray, were interrupted when the band had to play two outdoor festivals in Britain and Ireland. The album was finally completed on the eve of yet another world tour and Sting reflects that he had to be "dragged out of the house" to go back on the road.

The latest road venture for the band began on August 9 in Belgium and the European dates stretched through until the beginning of September. By the time Sting returned to Britain, his wife Frances had started a run at London's Old Vic theater in a controversial production of Macbeth that also starred Peter O'Toole.

A brand new Police single, titled *Don't Stand So Close To Me,* came out towards the end of September and, much to the band's (and A&M's) delight, it sold 500,000 copies in Britain during the first week of its release. The song's subject matter, which dealt with a schoolgirl's infatuation with a teacher, gave rise to a good deal of press publicity owing to Sting's pre-musical occupation. He told one reporter than he had been keen to write a song about sexuality in the classroom and

"If there is discovery, it's in challenge. Discovery is happiness."
—*Esquire, 1983*

that it had taken him over 18 months to get the hook. He admitted that he loved Vladimir Nabokov's novel *Lolita,* but claimed that, although he thought about it, he had never actually been guilty of "deflowering any virgins" during his teaching days.

The third Police album, ZENYATTA MONDATTA, finally surfaced at the beginning of October.

> **ZENYATTA MONDATTA**
> *Side One:*
> *Don't Stand So Close To Me*
> *Driven To Tears*
> *When The World Is Running Down,*
> *You Make The Best of What's Still*
>   *Around*
> *Canary In A Coalmine*
> *Voices Inside My Head*
> *Side Two:*
> *De Do Do Do, De Da Da Da*
> *Behind My Camel*
> *Man In A Suitcase*
> *Shadows In The Rain*
> *The Other Way of Stopping*

On the whole, the Lp contained a curious amalgam of material. Sting assessed that the record was put together too quickly and one can appreciate the difficulties of having to write songs in such a limited timeframe. He later told one critic that he like about a third of it—songs like *Don't Stand So Close To Me, When The World Is Running Down* and *Driven To Tears*—but declared, "the rest I would happily throw in the dustbin."

A week after the album was released, British fans were treated to a BBC television screening of *The Police In The East,* a documentary filmed by Derek and Kate Burbidge. The Burbidges, who have been responsible for quite a few Police videos, provided some excellent footage of the group's 1980 trek through Japan, Hong Kong, Egypt and Greece. A large portion of *Police In The East* can be seen in the commercial video *The Police Around The World,* which also showed the group in Australia, South America, France and Cairo.

In mid-October, 1980, the trio returned to live gigs with a couple of German dates. They spent the fall touring North America, where ZENYATTA MONDATTA made the Top 10 and *De Do Do Do, De Da Da Da* (Sting's effort to write about "the perversity of words and their dangers") became their first hit single since *Roxanne.*

The U.S. dates lasted until the first week of December, but by the final gig in Miami, Sting had picked up a virus. A South American mini-tour had been arranged and Miles Copeland was forced to cancel the Venezuelan shows. However, Sting was in good enough shape to play three nights in Argentina on December 14, 15 and 16.

"Money can't immunize me from the problems of the world. I'm sort of an industry, with accountants and lawyers and managers grabbing this bit of money, protecting that bit. Frankly, it all leaves me a bit cold. I quite enjoy having money and buying whatever I want, but if an MX missile explodes over my house, I'm as dead as the man next door."
—People Weekly, 1985

Less than a week later, the Police had come home to England, where they held three concerts in a giant tent that had been erected on Tooting Common in south London. It wasn't exactly an ideal venue and, due to the band's ever-increasing popularity, there were problems with overcrowding. Britain's *New Musical Express* commented: "Just because the Police have played in India, there is no reason to turn their Tooting Bec concert into a simulacrum of the Black Hole of Calcutta." A far more suitable venue was the 10,000-seat Bingley Hall, Stafford, where the trio performed on December 23.

Following a brief break over the Christmas holidays, the Police returned to America, where they sold out New York's prestigious Madison Square Garden on January 10. Midway through the set, a bottle was thrown onstage, which flew straight into Stewart Copeland's bass drum. While the kit was being fixed, Sting encouraged the crowd to join him as he sang "The Yellow Rose of Texas." He later commented that his ad-libbing had showed the band's human side and that the audience's participation helped to create an incredible sense of intimacy.

The next night, the Police played a "secret" gig at New York's Ritz club in front of less than 2,000 fans. During their stay in NYC, Sting also cut a version of Bob Dylan's *I Shall Be Released,* which was supposedly intended for a CBS television movie.

After leaving the Big Apple, the band flew directly to Los Angeles, where they headlined at the 15,000-seat capacity L.A. Sports Arena and also held another low-key club date this time at the Variety Arts Theater.

During a stopover in Miami, Sting went into a studio with producer Nigel Gray and recorded Spanish and Japanese versions of *De Do Do Do, De Da Da Da.* It marked Gray's last involvement with the Police; word has it that there had been problems with him during the ZENYATTA MONDATTA sessions and he had reportedly run into financial disputes with Miles Copeland over his fee. Sting actually hinted to the press that it might be time for the band to try working with a different producer and said that he wanted to have a strong-willed character— "a new sparring partner" as he termed it.

The U.S. tour had been completed at the end of January, after which they spent the month of February traveling through Japan, Australia and New Zealand. However, by March, the pressures of constant road life had begun to take their toll and the European leg of the tour was cancelled. The band finally came home and, according to Sting, they had reached the end of another chapter.

MAN OR MACHINE?

Although the Police had become hugely successful and continued to serve as an excellent vehicle for his songwriting, Sting was determined not to restrict himself to a shallow rock'n'roll existence. Towards the end of the trio's 1981 U.S. dates, he claimed that the only thing keeping him off drinking and taking hard drugs was his marriage, and that without his wife's "solid love, trust and affection" he would probably be a mental case. Contemplating his future with the group, he professed that he would stay while it was useful to his career and that as soon as it wasn't he would "drop it like a stone."

Rising to the status of international rock star may have been enough for a lot of people, but not for Sting. Consequently, as soon as the band had returned from their ZENYATTA MONDATTA tour, he started shooting the British televsion movie *Artemis 81*. Directed by Alistair Reid, it was filmed during the spring in England and Wales, with Sting playing the role of Helith, angel of love.

While Sting was busy filming, Virgin Books published a children's book, based on his song *Message In A Bottle*. Illustrated by Sharon Burn and Rosetta Woolf, it came in the shape of a bottle.

After three months hiatus, the Police regrouped at George Martin's AIR Studios on the Caribbean island of Montserrat in the second week of June. Sting had obviously decided that the band was still "useful" to his career. The recording sessions lasted just over a month and Hugh Padgham, who is best known for his work with the likes of Phil Collins and Hall and Oates, was on hand to help coordinate the production.

At the end of July, the trio flew to Caracas, Venezuela, for the two concerts that had been cancelled in December, 1980. Subsequently, they went to Canada to mix their upcoming Lp.

As soon as the record had been completed, Sting returned to England to start work on the film *Brimstone and Treacle*, which was based on a work by controversial British playwright Dennis Potter. In early September, he appeared at a charity benefit for Amnesty International called *The Secret Policeman's Other Ball*, which was held at

London's Theatre Royal on Drury Lane. Among the other artists to appear were Phil Collins, Jeff Beck, Eric Clapton and a host of British comedians. Sting played two songs—*Roxanne* and *Message In A Bottle*. A couple of weeks later, he jammed with the group Chelsea at a south London pub, reading his bass parts from notes that were supported on a music stool.

September also saw the U.K. release of the single *Invisible Sun*, which immediately raced to the top of the charts, despite the fact that its accompanying video clip was banned by the BBC. The promo film showed children playing in the streets of Northern Ireland, together with shots of British soldiers and military vehicles. Sting was upset; he recognized why the broadcasting authority had taken offence, but figured that it might have been a good chance to touch on an important issue through the popular music medium.

Discussing the lyrical content of the song in a press release, Sting commented: "I have a long association with Ireland. I married a girl from there and I get very upset by what's happening there. It was originally about Belfast and how people carry on normal life, but since I wrote it the conditions that exist in Belfast are happening in other British cities, only the kids haven't got a flag to wave."

Sting was obviously keen to release *Invisible Sun* in Britain, since he knew it would probably provoke controversy. However, the rest of the world received *Every Little Thing She Does Is Magic* as the first single from the forthcoming GHOST IN THE MACHINE Lp, which finally surfaced at the beginning of October.

GHOST IN THE MACHINE
Side One:
Spirits In The Material World
Every Little Thing She Does Is Magic
Invisible Sun
*Hungry For You (j'aurais toujours
    faim de toi)*
Demolition Man
Side Two:
Too Much Information
Rehumanize Yourself
One World (Not Three)
Omegaman
Secret Journey
Darkness

According to Sting, the album title was taken from a book by Arthur Koestler about comparative psychology, in which the author stated that man is becoming much more machine-like. Sting's point of view was that we shouldn't be like machines, since we are

"I am sort of two people . . . and I have a dark side."
—*The Tube, 1984*

more complex, more creative and more destructive.

GHOST IN THE MACHINE comprised an excellent selection of material and was a far better balanced album that ZENYATTA MONDATTA. Sting had afforded himself the time to work on some interesting lyrics and he aired a number of poignant messages on songs like *Spirits In The Material World, Too Much Information* and *One World (Not Three)*.

Commenting on *One World,* he stated: "We tend to think of the Third World as almost being another planet. The fact is that the problems they face now are the problems we will face soon. The sooner we think in terms of one world as opposed to three that we have artificially created, the better we are going to solve our problems."

As for *Spirits In The Material World,* he maintained that he had lost faith in the political process to solve the world's problems and that he was disillusioned with order.

On a musical note, aside from playing bass, Sting also contributed some saxophone on *Spirits.* He had originally picked up the instrument during his teens but had never taken it seriously. Shortly before the sessions for GHOST IN THE MACHINE, he invested in a new sax and reacquainted himself with the

playing technique.

Coinciding with the Lp's release, the Police embarked on a seven-date West German tour. They had added a New Jersey based horn section called the Chops, which gave the overall stage sound a considerable boost. Upon completion of the German gigs, Sting flew back to London to continue working on *Brimstone and Treacle.*

As they had done for the past two years, the band played a series of pre-Christmas shows for their British fans, which included three nights at Wembley Arena, one of London's biggest venues. December was a busy month for Sting, since he was also finishing off *Brimstone and Treacle* in between the U.K. gigs. During one shoot, he injured his hand after accidentally putting it through a plate glass window. Not to be deterred, however, he continued to perform with the band, going onstage with his arm in a sling and handing over his bass duties to a trusty member of the road crew.

The Police saw the calendar roll into 1982 with a New Year's Eve concert in

SAL
PRESS

Scotland. They then spent the next two weeks playing in France, Germany and Scandinavia, before kicking off a marathon U.S. trek in Boston on January 15. The first leg of their American tour dates ended a month later in San Francisco. Then followed concerts in Chile and Brazil, after which the group took a brief vacation in Rio de Janeiro.

The Police resumed their North American concert schedule with a show in Miami during the second week of March. The road trip ran through late April, when they played a string of New York area dates at venues like the Meadowlands and the Nassau Coliseum. On the eve of the first Meadowlands gig, Sting's wife Frances gave birth to their second child—a daughter, whom they named Fuchsia Katherine.

During the summer of 1982, Sting filed a lawsuit against Virgin Music in an attempt to regain control of the publishing rights to his early material, which he felt had been signed away unfairly. He maintained that the company had taken advantage of him when he was a struggling musician. Some of Sting's old diaries were actually read in court as evidence and Frances Tomelty also got up on the witness stand to testify for her husband. The case lasted for two weeks before an out-of-court settlement was eventually negotiated, with both Virgin and the songwriter claiming to have emerged victorious.

Within a few weeks though, the sensationalist British press was publishing reports that Sting and Frances' marriage was over. Always on the lookout for some celebrity gossip, the newsmen subsequently had a field day when they revealed that Sting had allegedly flown to the south of France, accompanied by "new girlfriend" Trudy Styler (with whom he has since had one child, with another due in May '85), to attend a party

given by the wealthy Adnan Khashoggi. Returning to Britain on a chartered jet, there was a scuffle with a vulture-like mob of paparazzi photographers, who were eager to take shots of the couple.

By the second week of August, Sting was back with the Police as they embarked on another series of North American concerts. The month-long tour climaxed with an appearance at the first Californian *US Festival*, which was held at a giant outdoor park near San Bernardino.

September also saw the British premier of *Brimstone and Treacle*. The movie marked his first major starring role on the silver screen and his performance earned favorable reviews. He played a "disturbed young man" named Martin Taylor and has claimed that he didn't have to delve too far into his own character when coming to terms with the role. "He's definitely an exaggerated version of me," Sting told one reporter. Talking about

the film in another interview, he confessed: "I'm very proud of it. It's quirky and weird and unusual. I'm not sure it's going to be a box office smash but then it isn't meant to compete with *Star Wars*."

The *Brimstone and Treacle* soundtrack album featured half a dozen solo cuts from Sting—*Brimstone and Treacle, Narration, Only You, You Know I Had The Strangest Dream, Brimstone 2* and *Spread A Little Happiness*. There were also three Police tracks, including the haunting *I Burn For You*, a song which Sting had originally written and performed when he was in Last Exit.

Spread A Little Happiness was issued as Sting's first solo single and naturally rumors began to circulate that his days with the Police were numbered. However, talking with Andy Summers in Los Angeles on the eve of the *US Festival* gig, the guitarist told me: "We're all doing our own things now and there's room for it—it's part of what comes

with being successful with something like the Police. It creates a platform to go off and do other things. So, Sting's done his film, Stewart has worked on a soundtrack for Francis Ford Coppola (*Rumblefish*) and I've worked with Robert Fripp.

"That's basically what we've all been up to this year and I expect we'll do more on our own in the future. But I can state quite categorically that the band isn't splitting and in fact the next major project for all of us is a new Police album, which we're going to start recording in December."

Andy's predictions proved correct and at the end of 1982 the Police set off to Montserrat, where they started working on their fifth Lp. December also saw the emergence of two more of Sting's solo recordings—his versions of the old classics *Tutti Frutti* and *Need You Love So Bad*—on the Dave Edmunds-produced soundtrack for the movie *Party Party*.

THE KING OF PAIN

An interesting discovery made while researching this project was a quote from Sting that appeared in a 1981 Police biography, titled *L'Historia Bandido*. Although the Police were riding high on the success of ZENYATTA MONDATTA at the time, Sting was clearly concerned about gathering new ideas for writing songs. He confessed that loneliness had played a key part in his previous work; he also claimed that he was grateful for some of the times he had been down in his life, times that had directly influenced songs like *So Lonely*, *Message In A Bottle* and *The Bed's Too Big Without You*.

He now needed fresh inspiration and confided: "This is scary. Do you know, I even cynically think about the day Frances and I might break up. I love her dearly, I mean I'm devoted to her and yet I can see how useful alienation is. If you're determined to be an artist you have to be hungry and my life now is too easy. I'm full. The artist in me is looking for death, for destruction. Artists are perverse. They're not normal. They ain't. I'm not normal."

Sting had, of course, broken up with Frances Tomelty by the time he started working on the Police's 1983 SYNCHRONICITY album. Somewhat ironically, the end of their seven-year marriage had a profound effect on what was unquestionably his finest work to date. As he later told *People Weekly:* "I'm grateful I went through the crisis. I worked hard to survive it. I grew. My best creative work so far is a result of trying to work out those problems." However, in another interview, he assessed: "In a sense I'm very suspicious of myself. I wonder if I manufacture pain in order to create."

Although Sting and the Police had begun work on SYNCHRONICITY in December, 1982, it wasn't until the following May that the first single from the Lp emerged. Titled *Every Breath You Take,* it was misinterpreted by many as a simple love song, but as far as Sting was concerned it was "a fairly nasty song that deals with surveillance, ownership and jealousy." He is said to have written the tune during a brief break in SYNCHRONICITY sessions when he went to stay at James Bond novelist Ian Fleming's house in Jamaica. Apparently, he woke up with the idea

"A sting is a little bit of pain . . ."
—1982

in the middle of the night, went straight to the piano and had the basic format worked out in 10 minutes.

As soon as *Every Breath You Take* was released, it became an international chart smash. A few weeks later, SYNCHRONICITY hit the streets.

> **SYNCHRONICITY**
>
> Side One:
> *Synchronicity I*
> *Walking In Your Footsteps*
> *O My God*
> *Mother*
> *Miss Gradenko*
> *Synchronicity II*
> Side Two:
> *Every Breath You Take*
> *King of Pain*
> *Wrapped Around Your Finger*
> *Tea In The Sahara*
> *Murder By Numbers*
> (cassette version only)

The album title was the result of Sting's fascination with C.G. Jung's concept of synchronicity. He felt that the psychologist's idea of a collective unconscious tied in well with the working relationship among the three Police members. It's no secret that there is an incredible amount of friction within the group, and Sting told *Musician* magazine that he though this was good "if it's a friction that doesn't come from ego. It should come from a passion about music. If I have an idea I believe in, I'll kill for it and I would hope that the others feel the same . . . that's where the tension and anger come in, and it's not a bad thing."

Once again, the majority of the songs on the album were written by Sting, with Andy Summers and Stewart Copeland contributing their token one song apiece. Chatting with Andy a couple of weeks before the Lp was released, I asked him whether Sting tends to have an overriding decision about the choice of material used. "Well, I don't know if it's an overriding decision," he replied. "But I think Sting has these tactics to gradually 'out' the songs. I can handle that as long as the material he has is very good. I don't always agree with the choice of material that goes down, but mostly Sting's songwriting tends to be so good that it's hard to argue. And I enjoy playing his material."

By the time SYNCHRONICITY was in the record stores, Sting had flown to Mexico, where he spent several weeks working on the set of *Dune*. In his eyewitness report, which appeared in the sci-fi/fantasy movie magazine *Cinefantastique,* writer Paul M. Sammon commented: "Sting is notorious for his formidable cool, a self-confidence which some say borders on arrogance. Watching from the sidelines, I don't see any of this. He's quiet and cooperative, a bit remote, but never a problem. Sting seems to be an erudite man whose sensitivity has been protected by an extremely well-constructed self-image. And, yeah, he's got that goddam rock star magnetism."

While he was in Mexico, Sting trained with martial arts' expert Kiyoshi Yamazaki for the film's deadly knife fight. As he later remarked: "One of the greatest things about making movies is that you develop some rather unusual skills."

Sting was back playing his "rock star" role on July 23, 1983, as the Police began another marathon world tour at Chicago's Comiskey Park. The subsequent North American concerts, which ran through the end of August, saw the trio playing a number of giant outdoor stadium gigs, including a show at New York's legendary Shea Stadium. Playing in front of an estimated 70,000 fans, Sting quipped: "We'd like to thank the Beatles for lending us their stadium!" He later confessed that he enjoyed the paradox of singing a song like *So Lonely* in front of such a huge crowd.

Upon completion of the U.S. dates, the Police traveled to Europe and finally brought 1983 to a close with a string of British concerts. Their protracted touring sting continued through the early months of 1984 and included a return visit to he U.S., together with a trip to Australia. Not surprisingly, SYNCHRONICITY became the group's best selling album, although Sting stated that he

was surprised by its commercial success, since he considered it their most "esoteric" output, particularly from a lyrical viewpoint.

Towards the end of their global trek, rumors were rife that the Police were on the verge of splitting up. Miles Copeland was forced to issue a statement in which he maintained that this was definitely not the case. However, it was quite clear that the band members would be allowing themselves time to work on solo projects before getting together again.

During the North American gigs, *Creem* had asked Sting whether he considered that being able to break away from the band and become involved in solo projects was almost therapeutic. "Yeah," he answered. "I mean the band is just one part of our lives. It's not the entire be-all and end-all of our lives. If it was, that'd be awful. I couldn't stand it. I need a private life, and I need private modes of expression."

Sting also told editor Dave DiMartino: "If you do go outside and do something else, it refreshes you, if anything. Otherwise a band can become a kind of prison, a sort of feudal system you can't get out of. Our band reserves the privilege and right to break up at any time. We can basically do what we want, there's no one holding a stick over us. And that allows me a sense of freedom, which I need."

Now that Sting had devoted a good deal of time to music, he decided to direct his attention to the film world. Not content with just one project, however, he committed himself to acting in a couple of movies—*The Bride* and *Plenty.* Consequently, he spent the rest of 1984 working in front of the cameras.

While a number of rock stars have attempted to make their mark in the celluloid world, very few have successfully crossed over from music to films. Sting seems to have accomplished the task, but he readily admits that it is a difficult transition. As he pointed out in *Interview:* "Most actors have a lot of time to train, to find out the skills of acting in relative privacy, whereas musicians spend all their formative years learning to play an instrument. Suddenly, you're offered a chance to be in a movie and you have to learn almost overnight how to act and also you have to do that in the glaring spotlight, on screen, in my case. It actually has its bonuses because the pressure is good for me. You have to learn—it's sink or swim basically."

The Bride, which is scheduled for a June '85 release, was directed by Franc Roddam, who was also responsible for *Quadrophenia.* He originally intended to offer Sting a cameo part, but after testing him backstage at a Police concert in Chicago he realized how much his acting abilities had grown and offered him the leading role of Dr. Frankenstein.

Discussing *The Bride* on a British television show, Sting revealed: "It's actually a sequel to *The Bride of Frankenstein*—it's not a remake. It's what happens after and it's done in the style more of Mary Shelley's original novel than the Hollywood invention of the 30's. It's not a horror film . . . it's a kind of fairy story really, where I become a monster. I make monsters for a living and I end up as a monster. It's also a *Pygmalion* story in that I've invented this girl, who I then teach how to behave in society. And it's

a love story."

Co-starring with Sting in *The Bride* was *Flashdance* leading lady Jennifer Beals. Apparently the couple exercised together while they were on location, and she informed *People* that he was "fun, sweet, supportive, and he didn't isolate himself in any way. Plus—he'd kill me if he heard me say this—he's in amazing shape for an old man." Much to the disappointment of the gossip columnists, there were no romantic links between Sting and Ms. Beals. According to Sting: "We didn't really say much to each other that wasn't scripted, though Jennifer's read enough to be able to talk about books. She's stimulating."

As soon as he had finished working on *The Bride,* Sting started shooting *Plenty* with Academy Award-winning actress Meryl Streep and the distinguished Sir John Gielgud. Sting maintains that working with such talented movie stars was both a privilege and an important landmark in his career. He still views himself as an "apprentice" in the film world, but reckons that actors get on well with him, once they realize that he's no drug-taking megalomaniac.

While Sting was busy filming *The Bride* and *Plenty,* the world was being inundated with advance publicity for *Dune,* which finally reached movie theaters in December, 1984. The celluloid adaptation of Frank Herbert's classic science fiction work had reportedly cost almost $60 million to make—the biggest-ever budget in movie history. Produced by Dino De Laurentiis, it was directed by David Lynch, whose previous credits include the quirky *Eraserhead* snd *The Elephant Man.*

Although Sting garnered a good deal of publicity for his involvement with the picture, he was only on screen for a few minutes. Appearing on *The Today Show* a couple of days before the movie opened, he stated: "I don't have a very large part in *Dune*—it's a cameo basically. I agreed to do it because I liked David Lynch's work so much; I still do. I find him an extraordinary man.

"The film is very strange. It's not like *Star Wars.* I think it's actually more original in its look and its appearance. A lot of the imagery and a lot of the ideas that were in *Star Wars* were taken from the book *Dune* by Frank Herbert. So, in a sense, it's the originator of a lot of ideas. But what's happened is David (Lynch) has taken it and moved it—or he's changed it. I think it looks great, I really do."

Sting may have liked the movie but, for the major part, it was panned by the press. In a particularly vicious review that appeared in the *New York Post,* noted film critic Rex Reed declared: "You only think you've seen rotten. Wait until you see *Dune.* This pretentious exercise in pointless insanity is so bad it's in a class by itself. It's diabolically bad." He went on to say: "After 15 minutes of gibberish, I gave up trying to figure out what the hell was going on and started snoring. There isn't a drug strong enough to get me through another experience like *Dune.* Not in this lifetime."

Iain Johnstone, film reviewer for the London Sunday Times, actually praised the cast, which featured Max Von Sydow, Francesca Annis and Kyle MacLachlan, and stated: "Sting too displays some polished pectorals in his fleeting presence. At the end of the film he has a brutal knife fight with the hero Paul." However, Johnstone questioned the credibility of the plot and concluded that the story was "impenetrable gobbledegook."

Aside from the release of *Dune,* December also saw the British radio presentation of two dramatizations based on Mervyn Peake's novels about the land of Gormenghast. Sting had actually acquired the screen rights a while back and written his own screenplay, intending to negotiate a movie deal. Eventually, he decided to put it out on radio.

Set in a castle, the story, according to Sting, "is about a kitchen boy, he's very clever and he works his way through the hierarchy till he's almost in control of the whole place. And it's about his eventual destruction through his pride and sense of evil. He's very like the character in *Brimstone and Treacle.* He's clever, but tainted by the devil."

The first part of Mervyn Peake's trilogy, titled *Titus Groan,* was broadcast on December 10. The following day, Britain's *Daily Telegraph* published a review, which proclaimed: "Sting, who is immediately more famous for being a pop star, is also a good actor. He shows himself in this (with the sequel *Gormenghast* to come next Monday) to have the exact vocal presence for his part and to possess the power to make the malevolent heart of the dark drama glow with eerie precision."

Now that he has earned acclaim for his

acting abilities in film, television and radio productions, one can only wonder whether Sting's next thespian endeavours will be on the stage.

Despite the fact that he spent much of 1984 concentrating on acting, he hadn't completely forgotten music. In fact, he had already begun to formulate ideas for his first solo record. Towards the end of the year, reports filtered through that he would be working on his Lp with IRS Records' trio Torch Song. However, by the beginning of '85, it was announced that the collaboration had proven unsuccessful. Word also had it that Sting was now keen to inject a strong jazz element into the project.

In mid-January, he flew to New York, where he assembled an impressive backing band that comprised Branford Marsalis, Kenny Kirkland, Darryl Jones and Omar Hakim. After a series of rehearsals, Sting returned to London and regrouped with the Police to attend the annual British Music Industry Awards.

The trio received a special presentation for their outstanding contribution to British music over the past seven years. The ceremony was held at London's Grosvenor House Hotel and, after accepting the award, Sting said: "We've been very lucky. We're a good team. We have a lot of talent and inspired management. To solve the problem of dividing the awards' trophy into three, we're giving it to Miles Copeland."

There has been a good deal of speculation that the next Police output might come in the form of a double live album. However, there have been a number of times where they have apparently started work on an in-concert release, but then shelved the idea in favor of another studio work.

When U.K. television reporter Paula Yates recently asked Sting about the band's future plans, he mused: "I don't know. I think it's very important not to just go out because the accountant says 'Oh, you better go and make a million bucks.' Because that way is stagnation as far as I'm concerned. I think the Police has to get back when we have a new idea or new way of presenting ourselves.

I don't want to just present the old formula, even though we know it works. That's not interesting."

A few days after the British Music Industry Awards, Sting was back in New York to continue working on his own album. During the last week of February, he played the three Ritz concerts before setting off to Barbados to start the recording sessions. According to an A&M Records' spokesperson, Sting's album is set for a late May/early June release. It will be interesting to guage the final results, since Sting has built up a strong reputation for continually coming up with something both exciting and innovative.

In a 1985 interview with *People Weekly*, he emphasized his desire to expand his overall horizons and stated: "I get every claustrophobic, very frustrated in one scene. My head can cope with more than one thing, and *needs* to, so I'm keen to get away from stereotypes and people's conceptions of what I am. I like people to be puzzled by what I'm doing next."
Expect the unexpected.

BY CHERRY LANE BOOKS

Now that you've enjoyed this edition of the ROCK READ series, here's your opportunity to check out all the other fine books in our catalogue. If you want the best biographies, fully illustrated of course, of today's top music stars, then simply send us your address and you will receive a free copy of the ROCK READ newspaper. With many official authorized biographies, you know you're getting the goods. Don't be fooled by cheap, inferior imitations, write to: ROCK READ, Dept. #8633 P.O. Box 190, Port Chester, New York 10573. Whether your taste in music is easy listening, new wave, country or heavy metal, if you want the best in rock reading - we've got it!